Learn to Draw

Disney·PIXAR
RATATOUILLE
(rat·a·too·ee)

REMY & EMILE IN PARIS

Adapted by Howard Father and Claire Williams
Illustrated by The Disney Storybook Artists
Inspired by the character designs created by Pixar Animation Studios

RATATOUILLE
(rat·a·too·ee)

Inside a cottage in the French countryside there lived a colony of rats. They kept to themselves in the attic of an old woman named Mabel.

One of the rats, Remy, possessed a highly developed sense of smell. He checked the rats' food from the old woman's compost heap to make sure it was safe to eat. But Remy had bigger dreams. He really wanted to be . . . a chef!

Remy's dad, Django, was proud of his son, the "food sniffer." But Django could not understand Remy's dreams about cooking food. So Remy kept his explorations in Mabel's kitchen a secret from everyone—except his brother Emile.

Emile didn't always understand his brother's odd behavior. And it made him very nervous when Remy started to read a cookbook written by his "favorite chef," Auguste Gusteau.

One day, as Remy and Emile sneaked into Mabel's kitchen for spices, Remy heard the TV announce that Gusteau had died. But before he could process the stunning news, the kitchen lights suddenly clicked on. Mabel had awakened! She nearly tore her whole house apart chasing after the rat brothers. Just as she had them trapped on the chandelier, the ceiling cracked and caved in—bringing the entire rat colony down with it! As Django led the rest of the rats to safety, Remy went back to get Gusteau's cookbook.

2

The rats jumped into their escape boats and headed down the river toward the sewer tunnels. Meanwhile, Remy escaped from Mabel's cottage and chased after his family. He used the cookbook as a raft and raced to catch up with the other rats, but he soon became lost in the tunnels of the sewer, all alone.

Then Remy heard a voice. It was Chef Gusteau, talking to him in his imagination! Gusteau told Remy to forget about the past; he encouraged Remy to leave the sewer and, instead, go up to the rooftop to see the sights. When Remy did what Gusteau suggested, he saw the beautiful night sky of Paris—and the bright sign of Gusteau's restaurant!

Remy peered through the skylight into the restaurant below. One of the cooks was introducing a tall, awkward young man named Linguini to Skinner, a tiny chef with an even tinier heart.

Linguini handed Skinner a sealed letter from his mother as he explained that he was looking for a job. Without reading the letter, Skinner reluctantly hired

Linguini as the garbage boy. But as Linguini began his new job, he knocked over a pot of soup! He tried to cover his mistake by pouring water and spices into the pot to make more.

Remy was so horrified at what he saw, he fell through the skylight. But as he ran to escape from the kitchen, he couldn't resist stopping and trying to fix the soup. He was busy adding a spice when Linguini caught sight of him. Rat and human stared at each other in shock. But before Linguini could do anything, a waiter whisked away the soup to the hungry customers.

Skinner was furious at the idea that Linguini was cooking! He was going to fire Linguini but changed his mind when he discovered that the customers liked the soup. Linguini was saved, but Remy wasn't—when Skinner saw the rat, he ordered Linguini to take it away and kill it!

Remy found himself trapped in a jar because Linguini didn't have the heart to throw him into the river. When Linguini started talking to himself, he was surprised to see Remy

3

nod back. Linguini couldn't believe that the rat not only knew how to cook, but he also understood humans! Linguini took Remy to his apartment.

The next day, Skinner demanded that Linguini make his special soup again. Remy hid under Linguini's hat, tugging Linguini's hair this way and that way to "steer" him to the correct ingredients. Before long, Linguini was chopping, mixing, and pouring. They were a cooking team!

Meanwhile, Skinner opened the letter from Linguini's mother. The letter said that Linguini was Gusteau's son, but Linguini didn't know—and Gusteau hadn't known either! According to Gusteau's will, Skinner would own the restaurant if no heir was found—but this letter said Linguini was an heir. Skinner's lawyer told him not to worry—Skinner could keep an eye on Linguini while he investigated whether Linguini really was Gusteau's son.

Skinner hated the thought of Linguini owning the restaurant. So he set up Linguini and a chef named Colette to cook the only truly disastrous

recipe Gusteau had created. Once Linguini failed, Skinner planned to fire him. Imagine Skinner's surprise when (thanks to Remy) the dish turned out to be a success!

Outside the restaurant, Remy was happily eating the good food Linguini had shared with him, when he heard a noise. It was Emile! The brothers reunited, and Emile took Remy to the rat colony's new home in the sewers.

All the rats cheered when Remy arrived. But Remy wanted to return to the restaurant and his job. Django encouraged his son to stay in the sewer, explaining that the world belonged to humans, and that all humans were enemies to rats.

Meanwhile, Skinner's lawyer confirmed that Linguini was Gusteau's son and rightfully owned the restaurant. Skinner decided not to share the news. He intended to keep the restaurant; he just had to make sure that Linguini didn't discover he was Gusteau's heir.

Skinner's plan might have worked if Remy hadn't

discovered Gusteau's will—along with the letter from Linguini's mother. Remy grabbed the papers with his teeth and ran through the streets of Paris as Skinner chased after him. Remy ended up on a boat, Skinner in the river.

When Skinner returned to his office, soaking wet and furious, he found Linguini with his feet up on the desk. The jig was up! Linguini knew he rightfully owned the restaurant, and Skinner was fired.

But with the change, Linguini started paying more attention to his newfound fame than to his cooking. Remy didn't like it, and neither did Colette. Linguini had forgotten his friends.

After a bitter argument with Linguini, Remy decided enough was enough. He told Emile to gather the entire rat colony and bring them to the restaurant. When Linguini returned to apologize, he saw Remy and the rats stealing food from the walk-in refrigerator, so he kicked them all out!

The next day, Anton Ego, the famous restaurant critic, sat down at Gusteau's and requested whatever "Chef Linguini" dared to bring him. Skinner lurked nearby, smirking. He couldn't wait for Linguini to fail.

In the kitchen, Linguini explained to his staff that Remy—who had returned to help

Linguini—was really the cook, not him. But the chefs didn't want to work with a rat, so they all walked out. Linguini would have lost everything—if it weren't for the rats. Django had seen Linguini stand up for Remy, and he decided this human was not so bad. He told all the rats to help. They didn't know how to cook, but they did whatever Remy needed, and together they saved the day!

Colette also returned, and she helped Remy make a simple dish called "ratatouille," which Linguini served to Ego. Ego took a nibble. He loved it! The delicious ratatouille brought back memories of his mother's cooking. The food critic finished every morsel of the tasty meal.

When Skinner burst into the kitchen to find out just who had made the ratatouille, he faced a kitchen full of rats—who tied him up!

Meanwhile, Ego asked to meet the chef, and Linguini presented Remy to Ego. Ego was shocked, but he still gave the restaurant five stars. He even helped open a new bistro, La Ratatouille, with a very special chef in charge of the kitchen. Remy's dreams came true: the little rat had become a real chef in a real bistro in the heart of Paris!

GETTING STARTED

Tools and Materials

Before you begin your drawing, you will need to gather a few simple tools. Start with a regular pencil so you easily can erase any mistakes. Make sure to have an eraser and pencil sharpener too! When you're finished with your drawing, you can bring your characters to life by adding color—just grab some colored pencils, markers, or even watercolor or acrylic paints.

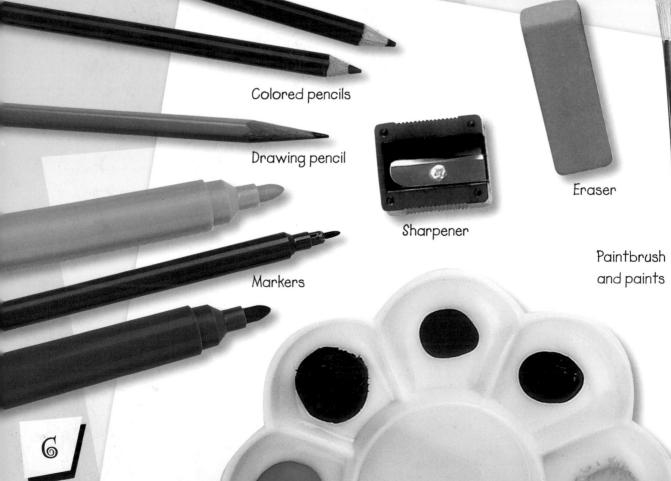

Colored pencils

Drawing pencil

Markers

Sharpener

Eraser

Paintbrush and paints

How to Use This Book

By following the simple steps below, you'll be drawing in no time!

STEP 1

Begin your drawing in the middle of your paper so you won't run out of room.

STEP 2

Each new step is shown in blue, so just draw all the blue lines you see.

STEP 3

Refine the lines of your drawing and add the details. Then erase the guidelines.

STEP 4

Now darken the lines you want to keep.

STEP 5

Finally, add vivid colors to bring your drawing to life on paper!

7

REMY

Remy is a little rat with big dreams. Born with a highly developed sense of smell, he can't stand eating garbage like the other rats, and he longs to become a gourmet chef. When Remy accidentally lands in the late, great Chef Auguste Gusteau's famous restaurant, Remy's dream just might come true . . . if he can remain hidden.

STEP 2

STEP 1

YES!
body leans
forward

NO!
doesn't tilt
backward

8

STEP 3

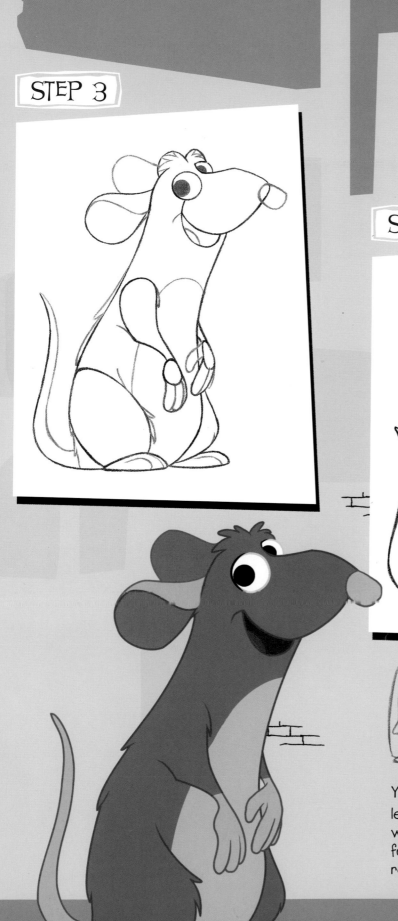

arm hair is ragged and loose

STEP 4

YES!
legs merge with body for a relaxed look

NO!
legs are not separate shapes

REMY

Remy likes to walk upright on two feet like a human, mostly because it helps keep his paws clean. Emile, his brother, constantly has to remind him to walk like a rat, so he won't get into trouble with their dad, Django. But Remy doesn't need a reminder when he's in a hurry. That's when his instincts take over, and he makes tracks on all fours!

STEP 2

STEP 1

YES!
ears are laid back

NO!
not tall and straight

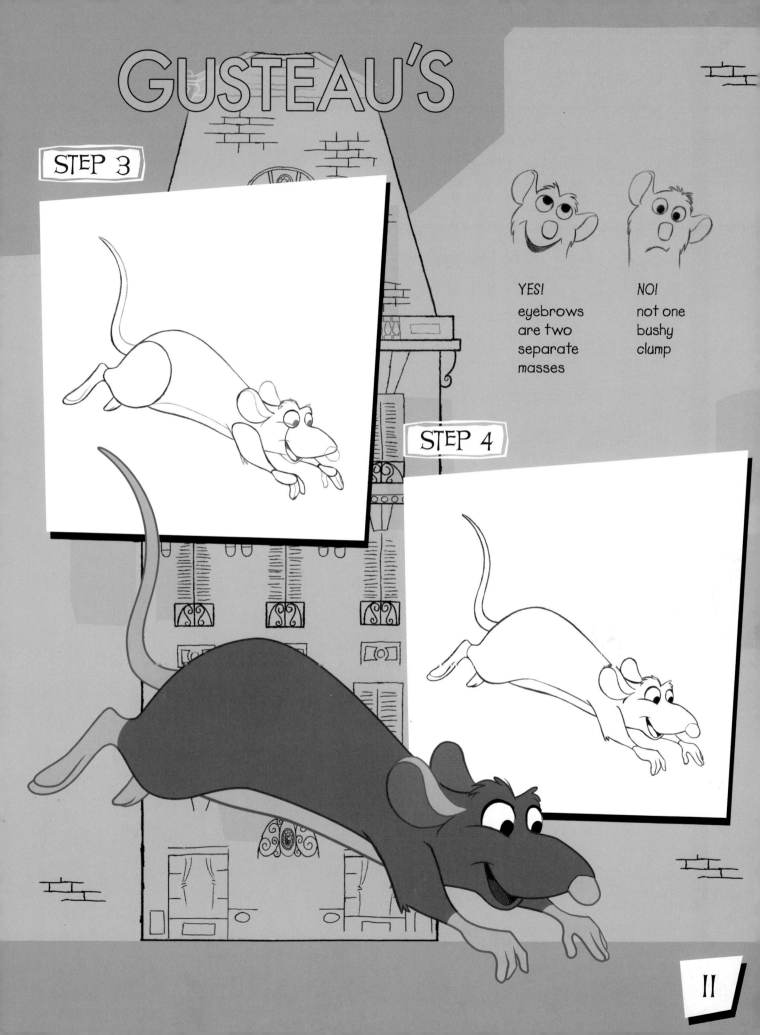

GUSTEAU'S

STEP 3

STEP 4

YES!
eyebrows
are two
separate
masses

NO!
not one
bushy
clump

11

EMILE

Remy's younger brother Emile is a rat's rat. He loves life—especially food, edible or inedible! Emile's also a little overweight. He's always good-natured, and he's always there for his brother. Even though he doesn't understand Remy's passion for good food, Emile's bottomless appetite makes him the perfect taste-tester for Remy's culinary creations.

big body but thin, delicate wrists

STEP 1

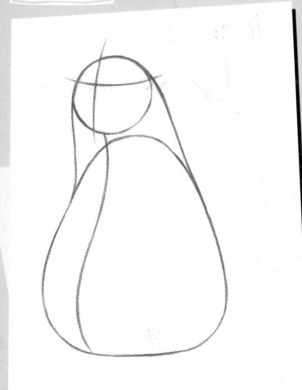

STEP 2

STEP 3

STEP 4

NO!
not large,
high, and
upright ears

YES!
Emile has small
ears that sit
low on head

13

REMY & EMILE

These two brothers are as different as night and day, especially when it comes to eating habits! But despite their differences, Emile and Remy get along well. They're genuinely delighted to see each other when they reunite outside Gusteau's restaurant.

STEP 1

Emile's belly is large and round

14

Emile's nose
curves up

Remy's nose
points down

STEP 4

DjaNGo

Remy's dad, Django, is the head of the rat colony. He is very proud that Remy is the group's "food sniffer," who makes sure their food is safe to eat. Django doesn't understand Remy's finicky tastes or his strange fascination with Gusteau's restaurant. To Django, humans are the enemy, and a restaurant kitchen is no place for a rat!

STEP 2

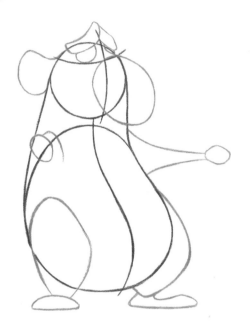

STEP 1

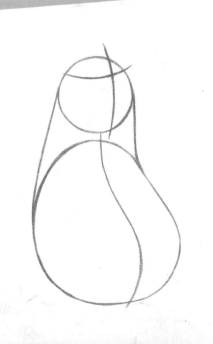

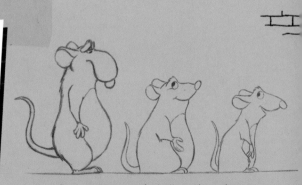

Django is much taller than his sons

eyebrows rest right on top of eyes unless he is surprised

STEP 4

YES!
fingers are round and smooth

NO!
not blocky and angular

17

THE BAND

One rat on the paperclip and another rat on the salt shaker are just the start of a full-on, swinging rat band that plays like crazy at Remy's welcome-home party.

STEP 1

STEP 2

STEP 3

YES! ears turn out and curve upward

NO! ears don't face forward

one is wide, the other thin

YES! tails taper to a point

NO! not round and even

STEP 1

STEP 2

STEP 3

19

LINGUINI

Linguini begins work at Gusteau's restaurant as a garbage boy, but an unexpected meeting with Remy gives him the chance to become a chef. Clumsy and timid, Linguini is an unlikely cook—especially because he knows nothing about cooking! Could his strange partnership with Remy actually succeed? *Mais oui!*

STEP 1

STEP 2

YES!
nose is big and round

NO!
not long and square

NO!
not small and pointy

STEP 3

STEP 4

YES!
arms curve at
the elbow

NO!
they don't
angle sharply

YES!
Linguini
has four
fingers
and a
thumb

NO!
not too
many
fingers!

GUSTEAU

Auguste Gusteau was France's greatest cooking genius. He authored *Anyone Can Cook!*, which inspired Remy to dream of becoming a chef. Gusteau's restaurant became famous thanks to his culinary vision—but Gusteau died (some say from a broken heart) soon after receiving a brutal review from Anton Ego, the food critic. Luckily, Gusteau's spirit lives on in his recipes—and in Remy's vivid imagination.

STEP 2

STEP 1

YES!
hat is tall and narrow

NO!
not wide and tapered

facial features sit high on
his pear-shaped head

STEP 4

Gusteau's body is
shaped like a lightbulb

23

SKINNER

Skinner is the chef in charge at Gusteau's restaurant. He's also next in line to become its owner. Small in height, and even smaller in heart, he won't let anyone get in the way of his plans to keep control of Gusteau's famous restaurant!

STEP 1

STEP 2

YES!
ear is flat on top and bottom, like a sideways U

NO!
not curved all the way around

GUSTEAU'S

STEP 3

STEP 4

YES!
thin
mustache
defines lip

NO!
not too
thick

Skinner's hat looks like
a salt shaker

COLETTE

The only female cook at Gusteau's, Colette is one tough chef. She is dedicated, talented, and hardworking. At first, she is resentful when she has to "babysit" Linguini and teach him everything she knows. But with time, Linguini's cooperative attitude and eagerness win her over.

STEP 1

STEP 2

Colette wears clogs in the kitchen

30

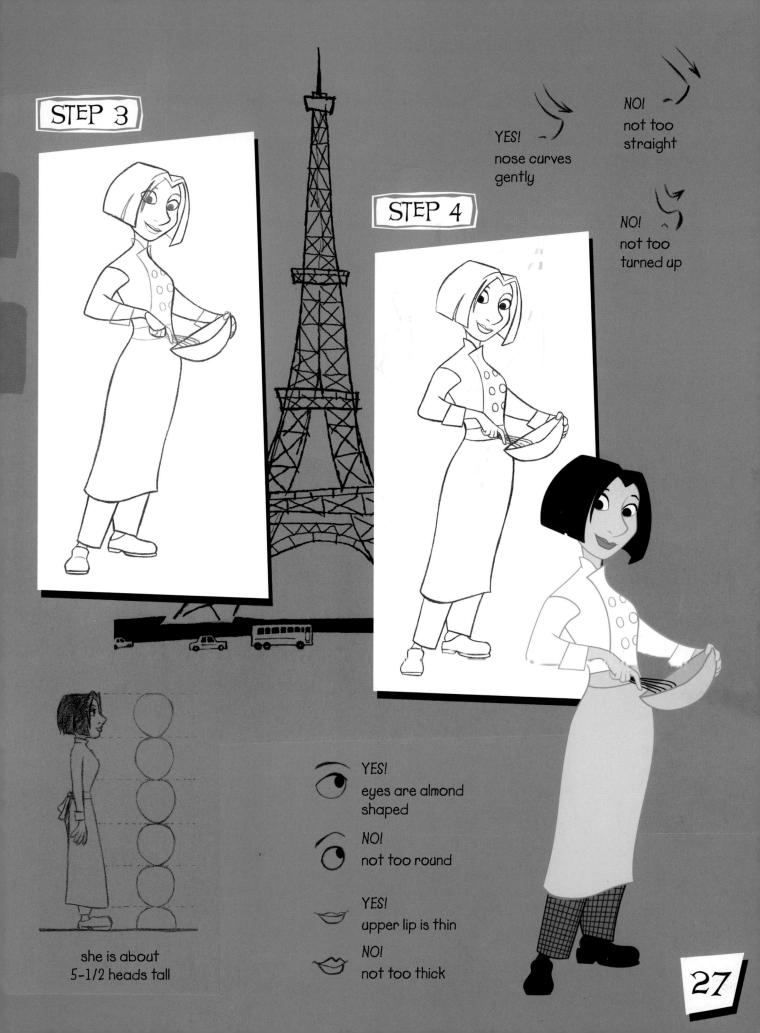

STEP 3

STEP 4

YES!
nose curves
gently

NO!
not too
straight

NO!
not too
turned up

she is about
5-1/2 heads tall

YES!
eyes are almond
shaped

NO!
not too round

YES!
upper lip is thin

NO!
not too thick

27

EGO

The most powerful food critic in Paris, Anton Ego can make or break a restaurant with a single review. Chefs are so afraid of displeasing "the Grim Eater" that no one dares change a menu without his blessing. When Ego hears that Gusteau's restaurant is popular again, he sets out to challenge the new chefs. Will it be *bon appétit* or bye-bye, Linguini?

STEP 1

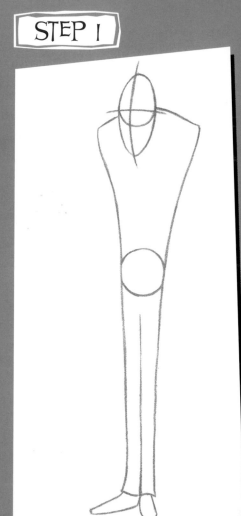

STEP 2

YES!
Ego's back is hunched and rounded

NO!
not straight

STEP 3

STEP 4

YES!
long upper lip
angles backward
into very small,
weak chin

NO!
upper lip not short;
chin not straight
and angular

YES!
large nose
is sharp
and pointed

NO!
not curved
and rounded

LINGUINI & REMY

Linguini and Remy form an unusual partnership that takes them on harrowing adventures inside and out of Gusteau's restaurant. In the end, their hard work and strange working habits pay off deliciously!

STEP 1

STEP 2

Linguini's head is shaped like an upside-down egg

STEP 3

STEP 4

Linguini's
chef hat

Linguini's
garbage
boy hat

Bon Appétit!

Now that you've learned how to draw Remy, Emile, Linguini, and the rest of their *amis*, you can try illustrating your own storybooks, greeting cards, posters, or wrapping paper. Anything goes, as long as you're having fun!